The Prude
Voltaire
Translation by William F. Fleming

Start Publishing PD LLC
Copyright © 2024 by Start Publishing PD LLC

All rights reserved, including the right to reproduce this book or portions thereof in any form whatsoever.

Start Publishing PD is a registered trademark of Start Publishing PD LLC
Manufactured in the United States of America

Cover art: Shutterstock/Taisiya Kozorez

Cover design: Jennifer Do

10 9 8 7 6 5 4 3 2 1

ISBN 979-8-8809-1957-4

Contents

Dramatis Personæ. 3
Act I. 4
Act II. 20
Act III. 36
Act IV. 49
Act V. 62

Dramatis Personæ

Mme. de Dorfise, a Widow.
Mme. de Burlet, her Cousin.
Collette, Chambermaid to Dorfise.
Blandford, Captain of a Ship.
Darmin, his Friend.
Bartolin, a Cashier.
Mondor, a Coxcomb.
Adine, Niece to Darmin, and disguised like a young Turk.

This comedy is partly imitated from an English piece, called the Plain Dealer. It does not suit very well for the French stage; the manners are too rough and bold, though much less so than in the original. The English seem to take too much liberty, and the French too little.

ACT I.

SCENE I.

Marseilles.

Darmin, Adine.

Adine: [Dressed like a Turk.] O my dear uncle, what a cruel voyage! what dangers have we run! and then my dress and appearance, too: still must I conceal under this turban my sex, my name, and the secret of my foolish heart.

Darmin: At last we are returned safe: in good truth, niece, I pity you; but, your father dying consul in Greece, both of us left, as we were after his death, without money or friends; your youth, beauty and accomplishments but so many dangerous advantages; and, to crown all our misfortunes, that wicked pasha desperately in love with you; what was to be done? you were obliged to disguise yourself, and make your escape as soon as possible.

Adine: Alas! I have yet other dangers to encounter.

Darmin: Dear girl, be composed, nor blush at what can't be prevented; embarking with me in such a hurry, and forced to disguise yourself in that manner, you could not with any decency resume your sex on board a ship before a hundred sailors, who were more to be feared than your old debauched pasha; but happily for us, everything has turned out well, and we are safely arrived at Marseilles, out of the reach of amorous pashas, near your friends and relatives, amongst Frenchmen, and good sort of people.

Adine: Blandford is certainly an honest man: but how dearly will his virtues cost me! that I should be forced to return with him!

Darmin: Your deceased father designed you for him: he had set his heart on that match when you were but a child.

Adine: There he was deceived.

Darmin: Blandford, my dear, when he is better acquainted with you, will do justice to your charms: he can never be long attached to a prude, who makes it her perpetual study to deceive and impose upon him.

Adine: They say she is handsome: he is constant in his nature, and will always love her.

Darmin: Constant! who is so, in love, child?

Adine: I am afraid of Dorfise.

Darmin: She has too much intrigue about her: her prudery, they say, has a little too much gallantry in it: her heart is false, and her tongue scandalous; never fear her, my girl, deceit can last only for a time.

Adine: Ay, but that time may be long, very long: the thought makes me miserable: Dorfise deceives him, and Dorfise has found the way to please.

Darmin: But, after all, niece, has Blandford really got so far into your heart?

Adine: He has, indeed; ever since that day, when the two Algerine vessels attacked us with such violence: O how I trembled for him! I think verily I was as much frightened for him as for you; I wished to be a man, indeed, that I might have defended him: don't you remember, uncle, it was Blandford alone who saved us when our ship was on fire? good heaven! how I admired his courage, and his virtues! they are deeply engraved in my heart, and never to be effaced.

Darmin: A grateful heart cannot but be prejudiced in favor of such distinguished virtue. I don't so much wonder at your choice: fine eyes, a noble demeanor, a good shape, and scarce thirty years of age, these are great recommendations to his—virtue: but then his strange humor and austerity can surely never be agreeable to you.

Adine: Why not? I am naturally serious myself, and perhaps in him may be fond even of my own faults.

Darmin: He hates the world.

Adine: They say he has reason.

Darmin: His temper is too easy and complying, he relies too much on others, and is too generous; and then his moroseness makes his freedom disagreeable.

Adine: The greatest fault he has, in my opinion, is his passion for Dorfise.

Darmin: That's too true; why, then, won't you endeavor to open his eyes, disabuse him, and shine in your true character?

Adine: How is it possible to shine in any character till we are able to please? alas! from the first day he took us both on board, I have been afraid he should discover me, and now I am on shore I have still the same apprehensions.

Darmin: I had intended to discover you to him myself.

Adine: For heaven's sake, don't; but join with me in my design upon him: sacrificed as I am to the adored Dorfise, I would wish to remain still unknown to him, and would have him continue a stranger to that victim which he offers up to love.

Darmin: What then is your design?

Adine: This very night to retire to a convent, and avoid the sight of an ungrateful man whom I cannot help loving.

Darmin: Indeed, niece, those who go to a convent in haste, generally live to repent it at leisure: I tell you, child, time will do all things: in the meanwhile, a more dreadful misfortune calls for our attention: the very instant that this new Du-Gué so nobly got off his ship, both his fortune and mine went to the bottom: we are both involved in the same calamity, and have come to Marseilles full of hope, but without a shilling! and must therefore look out for some immediate assistance: love, my dear niece, is not always the only thing to be thought of.

Adine: There, uncle, I differ from you; when you are in love, I think it is.

Darmin: Time will open your eyes: love, my dear, at your age is blind, but not at mine; and where there is no fortune, and nothing but grief and poverty with it, it has very few charms; only the rich and happy should be in love.

Adine: You think, then, my dear uncle, that now you are in distress you can have no mistress; and that your widow Burlet will forsake you as soon as she knows your circumstances.

Darmin: My distress perhaps may serve her for an excuse; such, my dear, is the custom of the world; but I have other cares to afflict me: I want money, and that's the most pressing calamity.

SCENE II.

Blandford, Darmin, Adine.

Blandford: So! so! in the age we live in everything may be had of everybody but money: what a heap of close embraces, kisses, fulsome compliments, false oaths, joyous welcomes, have I received from this whole city! but no sooner were they acquainted with my distress than every soul forsook me: such is this world.

Darmin: It is indeed a base one: but your friends come in search of you?

Blandford: Friends? know you any such? I have looked for them, and have found a number of scoundrels of every rank and degree: I have found honest men, too, that live in the bosom of indolence and plenty, like their own marbles, hard, polished, and always wrapped up in themselves, and their own interests; but worthy hearts, elevated souls, who were not the slaves of fortune, such as take a generous pleasure in relieving the unhappy, these, Darmin, I have seldom, very seldom met with: there is naught but vice and corruption on every side: Mammon is the god of this world; and I wish with all my heart, that all mankind had sunk with our vessel, and was buried in the waves.

Darmin: Be so good as to except me from your general sentence.

Adine: The world, I do believe, is false: and yet I think there is in it still a heart worthy of you; a heart that can boast of courage with sensibility, and strength with softness; which would resent the unkind treatment you have met with, by loving you, if possible, but the more for it: tender in its vows, and constant in its attachment to you.

Blandford: Invaluable treasure! but where is it to be found?

Adine: In me.

Blandford: In thee! away, deceitful boy, am I in a condition, think you, to listen to such idle tales? prithee, young man, choose a fitter time to jest in: yes, even in this world, I know there are pure and uncorrupted hearts, who will cherish my misfortune, and pity my distress: even in this low condition I have the happiness to reflect, that Dorfise at least knows how to love and to distinguish virtue.

Adine: Dorfise then is the idol of your heart?

Blandford: She is.

Adine: You have tried and proved her then?

Blandford: I have.

Darmin: My late brother, before he went to Greece, if I remember aright, designed my niece for you.

Blandford: Your late brother, my friend, made a bad choice then: I have made a much better: I have determined in favor of that virtue which, banished from the world, hath taken up its residence in the breast of my Dorfise.

Adine: Merit like hers is rare indeed; I am astonished at it, but, great as it is, it cannot equal her happiness.

Blandford: This youth is of a noble nature, and I love him; he takes my part even against you.

Darmin: Not so much perhaps as you think: but pray tell me, how happened it that this Dorfise, with all her attachment and love for you, never wrote to you for a whole year?

Blandford: Would you have had her write to me through the air, or the post travel by sea? I have received large packets from her before now, letters written in such a style too—so much truth, so much good sense, nothing affected, embarrassed, or obscure, no false wit, nothing but the language of nature and the heart; such is the effect of real love.

Darmin: [To Adine.] You turn pale.

Blandford: [Looking earnestly at Adine.] What's the matter with you?

Adine: With me, sir? O sir, I have got a sad pain at my heart.

Blandford: [To Darmin.] His heart! and what a tone, too! a girl of his age would have more strength and courage: I love the lad, but am astonished at his effeminacy: he was never made for such a voyage; he's afraid of the sea, the enemy, and every wind that blows: I caught him one day sitting down to a looking-glass: he appears to be cut out for the gay world, to sit in a box at a playhouse and admire his fine form, which he seems to be mightily enamored with: 'tis a very Narcissus.

Darmin: He has beauty.

Blandford: Ay, but he should beware of vanity.

Adine: You need not fear, sir, 'tis not myself that I admire: I am more likely to hate myself, I assure you; I love nothing that resembles me.

Blandford: Dorfise, my friend, is after all the mistress of my fate: convinced as I have long been of her prudence, I gave her a promise of marriage; at parting I left everything I had in her possession: jewels, notes, contracts, ready money, all, thank heaven, have I frankly trusted to my dear Dorfise; and her I consigned to the virtue of my friend, M. Bartolin.

Darmin: What! Bartolin the cashier?

Blandford: The same; a good friend, who esteems me, and whom I love.

Darmin: [In an ironical tone.] To be sure you have made an excellent choice, and are extremely happy in a mistress and a friend: not at all prejudiced.

Blandford: Not in the least: I am impatient at their absence, and long to see them.

Adine: [Aside.] I can bear it no longer: I must go.

Blandford: You seem disordered.

Adine: Everyone has some misfortunes or other; mine are heavy indeed, they overpower me, but they will cease—with Blandford's. [She goes out.]

Blandford: I know not why, but this grief affects me.

Darmin: 'Tis an amiable youth, and seems wonderfully attached to you.

Blandford: Blandford's heart is not a bad one, and what fortune I have, howsoever small it be, shall be in common with us both; as soon as Dorfise returns me the money I left with her, your young Adine shall have a part of it: I wish his voice was a little more masculine, and his air more easy: but time and care must form the manners of youth: he is modest, sensible, and has just notions of right and wrong. I observed through the whole voyage, that he would blush at any indecent expression which my people made use of on board: I promise you I shall endeavor to be a father to him.

Darmin: That's not what he wants of you; but come, let us go immediately to Dorfise, at least we shall get your money of her.

Blandford: True; but that unlucky demon which always accompanies me, has contrived to keep her in the country still.

Darmin: Well, but the cashier—

Blandford: The cashier is there, too; but they will both come to town as soon as they know I am here.

Darmin: You are satisfied then that Mme. Dorfise is always devoted to your service.

Blandford: Why should she not be? if I keep my faith to her, surely she may do the same by me; I have not been so foolish, as, like you, to throw away my heart on a gay coquette.

Darmin: It may happen that I shall find myself despised, but that you know every man is liable to; I will own to you, her airy, trifling humor is very different from that of her wise cousin.

Blandford: But what will you do with a heart so—

Darmin: Nothing at all: I shall hold my tongue, till our two fair idols make their appearance at Marseilles: apropos, here comes our friend Mondor.

Blandford: Our friend? said you! he our friend?

Darmin: His head no doubt is a little of the lightest, but at the bottom he is a worthy character.

Blandford: Prithee, undeceive thyself, dear Darmin, and be assured that friendship requires a firmer mind than his; fools are incapable of love.

Darmin: But the wise man, does he love so much then? come, we may reap some advantage from this fool notwithstanding; as the case now stands with us, there will be no harm in borrowing his money.

SCENE III.

Blandford, Darmin, Mondor.

Mondor: Morrow, morrow, my dears; so you are still in the land of the living: I'm glad of it, glad of it, with all my heart: good morrow to you; but pray, who is that pretty boy I saw in t'other room? whence comes he? did he come over with you? what is he, Turk, Greek, your son, your page, what do you do with him? where do you sup to-night, ha? boys, where do you throw your handkerchiefs? what! are you going post to Versailles to give an account of your battles? have you got ever a patron here?

Blandford: No.

Mondor: What, never made your bows at court?

Blandford: No: I made my bows at sea; my services are my patrons; the only artifices I make use of; I never was at court in my life.

Mondor: Then you never got anything.

Blandford: I never asked it; I wait till the master's eye in its own time shall find me out.

Mondor: Yes: and these fine sentiments will carry you, as they do everybody else, at their own time, to jail.

Darmin: We are pretty near it already, for our honor and glory has not left us a shilling.

Mondor: I am inclined to think so.

Darmin: Dear knight, let us fairly confess to you—

Mondor: In two words I must inform you—

Darmin: That our friend here has had a terrible loss—

Mondor: That I have made, my dear, a discovery—

Darmin: Of all his fortune—

Mondor: Of a famous beauty—

Darmin: Which he was carrying—

Mondor: To whom without vanity—

Darmin: By sea—

Mondor: After a good deal of mysterious conduct—

Darmin: In his ship—

Mondor: I have the happiness to be well with.

Darmin: This, sir, is a misfortune—

Mondor: O 'tis a most enchanting pleasure to conquer these excessive scruples, to get the better of that modesty, that fierce angry preceptor who is always thwarting and scolding at nature: I had once an inclination for Lady Burlet, for her gayety, and those pretty light airs she gives herself; but that was a foolish taste, as foolish as herself.

Darmin: I'm glad to hear it.

Mondor: O no, 'tis the prude I dote on: encouraged by the difficulty, I presented my apple to the beauty.

Darmin: Ay, sir, this prude, who has captivated your heart, this proud beauty is—

Mondor: Dorfise.

Blandford: [Laughing.] Dorfise! is it? O you know, I suppose, whom you are speaking to?

Mondor: To you, my friend.

Blandford: I pity thy folly, young man, and shall take care that, for the future, this lady shall never encourage such sparks as you.

Mondor: Very well, my dear: but let me tell you—your wise woman never complains when she is taken by a fool.

Blandford: Be so kind, however, my friend, as to play the fool no longer with her, for know, her virtues are destined to make me happy; she is mine, and has promised to marry me; she waits with impatience till we are united.

Mondor: [Laughing.] The pretty note that my friend, Blandford, has there! [To Darmin] you say he wants a few more in his distress; here, Darmin. [He is going to give him a pocketbook.]

Blandford: [Stopping Darmin.] Stay, take care, Darmin.

Darmin: Why, you would not—

Blandford: From him I would not—receive anything; when I do any man the favor to borrow of him, it shall be one whom I think worthy of it; it shall be a friend.

Mondor: And am not I your friend?

Blandford: No, sir: a friend indeed? an excellent friend who wants to run away with my wife; a friend who this very night perhaps would entertain twenty coxcombs at my expense: O I know them well; these fashionable friends, these friends of the world.

Mondor: That world, sir, which you grumble at, is better than all your ill-humor. Your servant, sir. I am going this moment to the fair Dorfise, to split my sides with laughing at your folly. [Is going off.]

Blandford: [Stopping him.] What say you, sir? Darmin, how is this? can Dorfise be here?

Mondor: Most assuredly.

Blandford: O heaven!

Mondor: And pray what is there in that so wonderful?

Blandford: In her own house?

Mondor: Yes, I tell you, at Marseilles; I met her just as I came in, returning in a violent hurry from the country.

Blandford: [Aside.] To meet me! thank heaven! now all my sorrows are past: come, I'll go, and see her.

Mondor: Done: with all my heart: the more fools there are, the more one laughs.

Blandford: [Going to the door.] I'll rap.

Mondor: Rap away.

Collette: [In the house.] Who's there?

Blandford: 'Tis I.

Mondor: 'Tis I myself.

SCENE IV.

Blandford, Darmin, Collette, Mondor.

Collette: [Coming out of the house.] Blandford! Darmin! amazing: lord, sir—

Blandford: Collette!

Collette: Bless me, sir, I thought you had been drowned long ago; you're welcome, sir.

Blandford: No, Collette; just heaven, propitious to my love, preserved me, that I might once more see thy dear mistress.

Collette: She is this moment gone out, sir.

Darmin: And her cousin, too?

Collette: Yes, sir, her cousin has gone along with her.

Blandford: But where, for heaven's sake, is she gone? where must I find her?

Collette: [Making a prudish curtsy.] At the—assembly.

Blandford: What assembly?

Collette: Lord, sir, you are mighty ignorant: you must know, sir, there are about twenty ladies of fashion most intimately connected to reform the age, to correct our foolish young women, to substitute in the room of that scandal which now prevails a prudent modesty and reserve, and Mme. Dorfise is at the head of the party.

Blandford: [To Darmin.] But how happens it, Darmin, that such a coxcomb as this should be suffered by so rigid, so severe a beauty?

Darmin: O prudes love coxcombs.

Blandford: Where does she go from the assembly?

Collette: That I can't tell: to do good in secret, I suppose.

Blandford: Secretly! that's the height of virtue; but when may I, in my turn, speak with her at home?

Mondor: That, sir, you must ask me; and I believe I may venture to grant it you: you may see her, sir, as you used to do.

Blandford: Your business, sir, is to respect her, and take care that you say nothing to her prejudice.

Darmin: And her cousin, too, pray where is she to be found? I was told they lived together.

Collette: They do so: but their tastes are different, and they are seldom together. Mme. de Burlet, with ten or a dozen young fellows, and as many pretty women, entertains herself every day, keeps a plentiful table, and goes forever to the comedy: afterwards they dance, or play; always at her house you will meet with good suppers, new songs, and bonsmots, old wines red and white, ice-cream, liquors, new ribbons, Saxon monkeys, rich bagatelles, invented by Hebert for the use of the fine ladies day and night, pleasures succeeding pleasures; scarce is there a moment left even to scandalize one another.

Mondor: Ay, this, my friend, is the way to live.

Darmin: But whither must I follow her?

Collette: Everywhere; for she runs about from morning to night, and sees everything; plays, balls, music, suppers; she is always employed: perhaps very late in the evening you may meet with her and her joyous companions at home, about supper-time.

Blandford: If, after what I have heard, you are fond of her, my friend, you must have as little understanding as herself; is it possible to love a woman, who has all the follies of her sex put together? to be sure, it will be worth your while to follow her chariot wheels, to dance after a coquette, and sigh and whine for a ridiculous creature who thinks of nothing but her pleasures.

Darmin: I may be mistaken, but I cannot help thinking that a love of pleasure, and the strictest honor, may be consistent with each other; and I am likewise of opinion, with all due deference to you be it spoken, that a prude, with all her severity of virtue, may do a great deal of good in public, and yet in secret is often good for—just nothing.

Blandford: Well, well! we shall be better judges by and by; you shall see my choice, and I yours.

Mondor: Ay, ay, by the time you return, my dears, the place will be taken.

Blandford: By whom, pray?

Mondor: By me.

Blandford: By you?

Mondor: I have made too good use of your absence to be afraid of your presence, I assure you: so fare you well.

SCENE V.

Blandford, Darmin.

Blandford: Well, what think you? can one be jealous of such a creature?

Darmin: O fools have fortune, you know: nothing more common.

Blandford: You can never imagine, surely—

Darmin: O yes: your sensible women are very fond of fools at times: but I must take my leave, to know my own fate, and see whether I am a happy or a forsaken lover. [He goes out.]

Blandford: [Alone.] Ay, ay, make haste, and get your dismissal: poor fellow! I pity him: how happy am I to have made choice of a woman worthy of my esteem! unfortunate as I have been, I have reason to bless the hour of my return: reason increases my passion: yes: I am resolved; I will leave the world, the whole ungrateful world, for one good and worthy woman. I have had enough of hopes and fears: the port at length appears, and there will I shelter myself: what is all the world to this? a foolish, ridiculous, fatal world! ought I not to detest it? there is not a friend remaining in it; not a creature, who at the bottom really cares a farthing for one: O 'tis a vile world: if there is any love or affection to be expected, it must be from a wife; all the difficulty is how to choose one. A coquette is a monster one would avoid, but a beautiful, a tender, and a sensible woman, is the noblest work of nature.

ACT II.

SCENE I.

Dorfise, Mme. De Burlet, Mondor.

Dorfise: I must beg of you, M. Mondor, not to indulge yourself in this excessive familiarity: it is impossible for ears so chaste as mine to suffer such liberties.

Mondor: [Laughing.] And yet you like them: you rate me for my impertinence, but you listen to it: why, my dear, your hair is cut short on purpose, that you may hear the better.

Dorfise: Again?

Mme. De Burlet: Indeed I shall take his part: you are too rigid, and affect too much severity: liberty is not always licentiousness; there is nothing indecent, in my opinion, in little sallies of innocent mirth and gayety, which we may choose whether we will understand or not; but your outrageous virtue would shut up our mouths and our ears together.

Dorfise: I would indeed, cousin: and moreover, I would advise you to shut your doors, too, against some visitors whom I frequently see here; I have told you often enough, cousin, it will ruin your reputation: how can you suffer such a libertine crew? Cleon, that pretty fellow, who is very brilliant without a spark of wit, and is always laughing at the good things he would make you believe he has just said; Damon, who for twenty beauties that he is in love with, makes twenty madrigals as insipid as himself; and that Robin, who is always talking of himself, with the old pedant that makes every creature sick of him: then there's my cousin, too, that—

Mondor: Enough, enough, madam: let everybody speak in his turn; and since your ladyship shows so much good nature in speaking of the world, I will endeavor to convince you I have at least as much charity as yourself, and propose giving you in three words a picture of the whole city: to begin then with—

Dorfise: Stop thy licentious tongue: none should dare to chastise vice but persons of the strictest virtue; I cannot bear to hear libertines satirizing others who are much less culpable than themselves; for my part, what I say is from my regard to the honor of human nature, and disgust of the world, this vile world: how I do hate it!

Mme. De Burlet: For all that, cousin, it has some attractions.

Dorfise: For you, I believe it has, and to your ruin.

Mme. De Burlet: And has it none for you, cousin? do you really hate the world?

Dorfise: Horribly.

Mme. De Burlet: And all the pleasures of it?

Dorfise: Abominably.

Mme. De Burlet: Plays? balls?

Mondor: Music, dancing—

Dorfise: O my dear, they are all the devil's inventions.

Mme. De Burlet: But dress and finery? you must acknowledge—

Dorfise: All vanity! O how I regret every minute thrown away at my toilette! I hate to look at myself; and, of all things in nature, detest a looking-glass.

Mme. De Burlet: And yet, my dear rigid cousin, you seem tolerably well dressed.

Dorfise: Do I?

Mondor: Extremely well.

Dorfise: Plain, very plain.

Mondor: But with taste.

Mme. De Burlet: You may say what you please, but your wise ladyship loves to please.

Dorfise: I love to please? O heaven!

Mme. De Burlet: Come, come, be honest; have you not some small inclination to this young rattle? he's not ill made. [Pointing to Mondor.]

Mondor: O fie!

Mme. De Burlet: Young, rich, and handsome.

Mondor: Pooh, prithee.

Dorfise: O abominable! a handsome young man is my aversion; handsome and young! O fie, fie!

Mondor: Upon my soul, madam, I am concerned for both of us; the wicked woman to talk so: but pray, madam, this Blandford, who is come back without his ship, is he so rich, and young, and handsome?

Dorfise: Blandford? why, is he here?

Mondor: Certainly.

Collette: [Entering hastily.] O madam! I come to tell you—

Dorfise: [Whispering to Collette.] Hark'ee.

Mme. De Burlet: How's this?

Dorfise: [To Mondor.] I thought since he took his leave of me he had been cured of all his faults; to tell you the truth, I imagined he was dead long ago.

Mondor: No, madam, he is alive, I assure you: the pirate intends to sink me at once: he pretends to be a favorite of yours.

Dorfise: [Aside to Collette.] O Collette!

Collette: O madam!

Dorfise: [To Mondor.] Dear sir, can't you find out some means of sending him to sea again?

Mondor: O yes: with all my heart.

Mme. De Burlet: Pray, sir, is there any news of his intimate friend and confidant, Darmin? has he arrived?

Mondor: He has, madam: the captain it seems fell in with him at some port or other: they have had a battle at sea, and now are returned home without a stiver; Blandford has brought with him a little Greek, too, the handsomest, genteelest—

Dorfise: O yes: I believe I saw him just by my house: large black eyes?

Mondor: The same.

Dorfise: Penetrating, yet full of softness: rosy cheeks?

Mondor: He has so.

Dorfise: Fine hair, and teeth: something in his air that's noble and fine?

Mondor: The very paragon of nature.

Dorfise: If his morals are good; if he is well-born and discreet, I'll see him: you shall bring him to me—though he is young.

Mme. De Burlet: I must find out Darmin's lodging as soon as possible: here, la Fleur, go this minute and carry him these five hundred pounds, [she gives a purse to la Fleur] and tell him I expect Blandford and him to supper with me: our friends have long wished for his return, and none more than myself; never did I know a better creature, more honest, or ingenuous: I admire above all things his amiable complacency, and those social virtues that so strongly recommend him.

Dorfise: Blandford is not of his disposition: he is so serious.

Mondor: So full of spleen!

Dorfise: True, and so jealous!

Mondor: So affronting!

Dorfise: He is—

Mondor: Very true.

Dorfise: Let me speak, sir; I say he is—

Mondor: Yes, madam, I attend to you—he is—

Dorfise: He is in short a dangerous man.

Mme. De Burlet: They tell me he has fought nobly for his king and country, and distinguished himself greatly at sea.

Dorfise: That may be, cousin, but by land he is dreadfully troublesome.

Mondor: And besides he is—

Dorfise: True.

Mondor: O those sailors have all of them such horrid principles.

Dorfise: They have so.

Mme. De Burlet: But I have heard, cousin, that you formerly gave him some hopes—

Dorfise: Yes: but since that I have taken an antipathy to the whole world, and quitted it: I began with him; 'twas he and the world together that have made me so fearful.

SCENE II.

Dorfise, Mme. De Burlet, Mondor, Collette.

Collette: Madam!

Dorfise: Well!

Collette: M. Blandford has come.

Dorfise: O heaven!

Mme. De Burlet: Is Darmin with him?

Collette: Yes, madam.

Mme. De Burlet: I am heartily glad of it.

Dorfise: And I'm heartily sorry; I must retire; I would fly from the whole world.

Mondor: With me, I hope.

Dorfise: No, sir, if you please, without you. [She goes out.]

SCENE III.

Mme. De Burlet, Blandford, Darmin, Mondor, Adine.

Darmin: [To Mme. de Burlet.] Permit me, madam, at length on my knees—

Mme. De Burlet: [Running up to Darmin.] O my dear Darmin, come along, I've made an engagement for you to go to the ball when the comedy is over: we'll prate as we go along; my chariot's below. [To Blandford.] And you, M. Solemnity, will you come with us?

Blandford: No: I came here, madam, on a serious affair: away, ye train of triflers, go, and pretend to pleasures which you never enjoy; go, and be weary of one another as soon as you can: you and I [turning to Adine] will go in search of Dorfise.

SCENE IV.

Blandford, Adine, Collette.

Blandford: Then we shall see a woman indeed; a woman submitting to every duty of life; a woman who for me has renounced the whole world; and who to her faithful passion joins the most scrupulous and rigid virtue: I hope you will endeavor to recommend yourself to her.

Adine: Of that, sir, you may assure yourself; I shall try to imitate her virtues; her example may be the best instruction to me.

Blandford: I'm glad to hear you think so: I'll introduce you to her: from this time forward I shall look upon you, Adine, as a son whom fortune has thrown in my way, to make amends for all her past unkindness; it is impossible to know without loving thee; your disposition is only too pliant and flexible; nothing therefore can be of more service to you than to keep company with a prudent and discreet woman, whose acquaintance will improve the goodness of your heart, and confirm you in your honesty, and love of justice, without depriving you at the same time of that sweetness and complacency which I own I find myself deficient in: a woman of sense and beauty, who has nothing trifling or ridiculous in her, is an excellent school for a young fellow at your time of life; it will form your mind, and direct your heart; her house is the temple of honor.

Adine: The sooner we visit it then the better; but her example is so uncommon, I fear I shall never be able to follow it.

Blandford: Why not?

Adine: Because I like yours better: there is something in your virtue, though the external appearance has too much severity in it, that charms me: it must, I am sure, be good at the bottom: you have always been my favorite, but for Dorfise—

Blandford: [Going towards the door of Dorfise's house.] You must not indeed flatter yourself that you can at once be able to imitate her; but in time you may: however, let me advise you to see Dorfise, and to avoid her cousin. [He is going in, Collette comes out, stops him, and shuts the door; he knocks at it.]

Collette: You must not go in, sir.

Blandford: Not I?

Collette: No, sir.

Blandford: How's this, Blandford refused admittance?

Collette: My mistress, sir, is retired to her apartment, and would be private.

Blandford: I admire her delicacy, but I must go in.

Collette: Pray hear me, sir.

Blandford: Not I: I will go in, and this minute too. [He goes in.]

Collette: Stay, sir.

Adine: I'll follow him and see the event of this strange interview.

SCENE V.

Collette: [Alone.] Now will he see her, and discover all: I'm frightened to death about it: 'twill be all over now with my poor mistress: what a foolish woman! to stipulate this secret marriage, and give herself to such a fellow as Bartolin: what will the malicious world say? well; women are strange creatures, that's the truth of it: nay, and so are the men too: what excessive weakness! to be sure my mistress is a fool; she deceives herself and everybody else; and half her time is employed in finding out artifices to hide her indiscretion, and repair her reputation. She follows her inclination, and then has recourse to intrigue and management, and yet she takes no care of the main point: this is a cursed adventure for us, and a most unfortunate return: how will Blandford take the injury she has done him? here have we no less than three husbands in the house, two of them promised, and the other, I believe, absolutely taken: a woman in such a case must be a little hampered.

SCENE VI.

Dorfise, Collette.

Collette: O madam, what's to be done?

Dorfise: Fear nothing; there are ways and means to dazzle people's eyes, to delay, and put off matters; men are easily managed, their weakness is our strength, and helps our designs against them: I have got myself out of the worst scrape: our disagreeable interview is over—and I have sent the good man—God speed him—into the country to his old crony Bartolin. who may lend him some money; at least I shall gain time by it, and that's enough.

Collette: But surely, madam, the deuce was in you to sign that plagued contract! what had you to do with Bartolin?

Dorfise: The devil, my dear, is full of spite, that's certain: that fellow persecuted me so: but we tempt, and are tempted, and the heart easily surrenders: you know we heard that Blandford would never come back again.

Collette: That he was dead.

Dorfise: I was left without any support, money or friends, and weak withal: all owing to the weakness of my sex, Collette; but our stars will prevail: 'tis often the lot of a beauty to marry a scab: my heart was severely attacked.

Collette: There are certain seasons very dangerous to a prude: but if you must sacrifice to love, you should have taken the chevalier, he is handsome.

Dorfise: O but I wanted a bit of intrigue and mystery, besides I am not fond of his character: but he is useful to me: he is my puffer, my emissary: he's a prate-apace you know, and can scatter reports about town for me that may be serviceable.

Collette: But Bartolin is such a villain.

Dorfise: Yes, but—

Collette: And for his wit, I'm sure there are no charms in that.

Dorfise: No: but—

Collette: But what?

Dorfise: Fate, whim, caprice, my unhappy circumstances, a little avarice withal, and then opportunity—in short, I surrendered, played the fool, and signed the contract. I kept, you know, Blandford's strong box, and after he was gone, gave away a little of his money for him—out of charity: who would ever have thought, that, after two years, he should be constant to his old flame, and come back again to look for his wife and his strong box?

Collette: Everybody here said he was dead, and now he is not; the fellow's a fool, and stands in his own light.

Dorfise: [Resuming the Prude.] Well, since the man's alive, I must give him his jewels back: let him take them: but Bartolin has got them to keep for me; he fancies they are mine, holds them fast, and is fond of them and as jealous as he is of me.

Collette: So I suppose.

Dorfise: Husbands, jewels, virtue, and character, how to reconcile you all, heaven knows!

SCENE VII.

mondor, adine, dorfise.

Mondor: I must drive away this powerful rival, who gives himself such airs, and despises me; positively must.

Adine: [Coming in slowly.] What's this? I'll listen a little.

Mondor: In short, I must make myself happy, and punish his insolence: 'tis you, 'tis Dorfise alone whom I adore: let old Darmin enjoy his little coquette, they are not worth our notice: but Blandford, the severe and virtuous Blandford, there I own I could wish to triumph: he thinks you can refuse him nothing, because he is a man of honor and virtue: now to me these are the most disagreeable creatures in the universe; indeed, my queen, you'll soon be heartily tired of him.

Dorfise: [Prudishly, after looking steadfastly at Adine.] You are mistaken, sir: I have the highest respect and esteem for M. Blandford.

Mondor: There are those, madam, whom one may esteem, and yet laugh at, and make fools of: is it not so?

Adine: [Aside.] Amazing! she is constant and virtuous: doubtless she loves him: I am confounded: who would have thought it?

Dorfise: What is he talking of?

Adine: [Aside.] Dorfise is faithful, and, to complete my misery, she is handsome.

Dorfise: [To Mondor, after looking tenderly at Adine.] He says, I am handsome.

Mondor: There he's right: but he begins to be troublesome: hark'ee, child, I have something to say to this lady in private.

Adine: I will retire, sir.

Dorfise: [To Mondor.] I say, sir, you are greatly mistaken. [To Adine.] Stay you here, my dear. [To Mondor.] How dare you, sir, send him away? [To Adine.] Come hither, child: he's almost ready to weep; the sweet boy! he shall stay with me: Blandford brought him to me; and from the first moment I took a fancy to him: I like his disposition.

Mondor: O let his disposition alone, for heaven's sake, and attend to me: this Blandford, madam, I know you hate him: you have often told me he is brutal, jealous—

Dorfise: [Angrily.] Never, sir. [To Adine.] What age are you?

Adine: Eighteen, madam.

Dorfise: Such tender youth as thine requires the curb of wisdom to guide and direct it: vice is bewitching, temptations frequent, and example dangerous: a single glance may be your ruin; be upon your guard against women, nay, and against yourself, and dread the poisonous blast that withers the sweet flower of virtue.

Mondor: Prithee, Dorfise, let the boy's flower alone: what is it to you whether it be withered or not? mind me, my dear.

Dorfise: My God! his innocence is so engaging!

Mondor: 'Tis a mere child.

Dorfise: [Coming up to Adine.] What's your name, my dear, and whence come you?

Adine: My name, madam, is Adine; I was born in Greece: M. Blandford brought me over with Darmin.

Dorfise: 'Twas kindly done of him.

Mondor: What a ridiculous curiosity! here I am making strong love to you, and you all the while talking to a child.

Dorfise: [Softly.] Be quiet, you blockhead!

SCENE VIII.

Dorfise, Mondor, Adine, Collette.

Collette: Madam.

Dorfise: Well!

Collette: They wait for you at the assembly.

Dorfise: Well: I shall be there presently.

Mondor: Hang your engagement: I tell you what, my dear; you and I will put an end to these prudish meetings, these conspiracies against love, taste, and gayety: upon my word, child, it does not become a beautiful young creature, as you are, to go about declaring against everything that's joyous, amongst a parcel of toothless old beldames, that meet together in their gloomy vaults to weep over the pleasures of the living: but I'll go and rout these immortal tattlers, and stop their clack with a hundred bon-mots.

Dorfise: For heaven's sake, don't go and expose me there, I desire you: positively you shall not.

Mondor: Positively I will, this minute, and tell them you are coming. [He goes out.]

Dorfise: The wild creature! [To Adine.]

Avoid, my dear, whatever you do, such fools as these: be prudent, and discreet: make my compliments to Blandford—what a piercing eye!

Adine: [Turning back.] Did you speak, madam?

Dorfise: That sweet complexion! that ingenuous look! so charming! so modest!—I hope I shall have the pleasure of seeing you often.

Adine: I shall pay my respects, madam, with the greatest pleasure: madam, your servant.

Dorfise: Adieu, my dear child.

Adine: I don't know what to think of it: I can't discover whether she deceives him or not; all I know is, I love him.

SCENE IX.

Dorfise, Collette.

Dorfise: [Looking after Adine.] What said he? I love! love whom? perhaps the boy has fallen in love with me; he talks to himself, stops, and looks at me; I have certainly turned his brain.

Collette: He ogles you most wonderfully, and looks with such tenderness.

Dorfise: Is that my fault, Collette? how can I possibly help it?

Collette: Very true, madam: but danger approaches: I am terribly afraid of this Blandford's coming back again, and dread still more the savage resentment of Bartolin.

Dorfise: [Sighing.] This young Turk's mighty handsome! do you think he is a Turk? that an infidel can have such softness in his manner, so fine a figure? I fancy I could convert him.

Collette: I'll tell you what I fancy: that when it is discovered you are married to Bartolin, your reputation will be severely handled: Blandford will storm dreadfully, and your little Turk will be of no great service to you.

Dorfise: Never do you fear.

Collette: I have long, madam, relied on your prudence: but Bartolin is a jealous brute, and what's worse, he is—your husband: 'tis really a melancholy case, and indeed rather singular: the two rivals, I am afraid, will be very intractable.

Dorfise: O I can avoid them both: peace is the object of my wishes: it is my duty and my interest to foresee and prevent the ill consequences of a discovery; I have friends, men of merit and fortune.

Collette: Take their advice.

Dorfise: I intend to, immediately.

Collette: But whose?

Dorfise: Why, let me see—suppose I ask this stranger—this little—

Collette: Ask his advice? the advice of a beardless boy?

Dorfise: He seems to be very sensible, and if he is, why not consult him? let me tell you, young people are the best counsellors in things of this kind: he might throw some light on my affairs; besides, he is Blandford's friend, and I must talk with him.

Collette: O to be sure, madam, 'tis quite necessary.

Dorfise: And as one talks over such things better at table, it would not be amiss to ask him to dinner: what think you?

Collette: Softly there, madam: excuse me, but you who are so afraid of scandal—

Dorfise: I am afraid of nothing: I know what I am about: when once a reputation is established, we may be perfectly easy about it: all the party will defend us, and cry out on our side.

Collette: Ay, but the world will talk, madam.

Dorfise: Well! for once we'll submit to the wicked world: I'll give up this innocent dinner, and not sharpen their malicious tongues: I'll talk no more with Adine, never see him again; and yet, after all, what could they say of a child? but to chastity and virtue I will add the appearance of them also; will observe decency and decorum: I'll do it in my cousin's name, and beg her—

Collette: An excellent contrivance! a woman of the world has no reputation to lose; one may put her name to ten billets-doux; she may have as many lovers, as many assignations as she pleases: nobody's offended, nobody blushes, nobody's surprised: but if, perchance, a lady of honor makes a false step, it must be carefully concealed.

Dorfise: A false step! I make a false step! thank heaven! I have nothing to reproach myself with: to be sure, I have signed, but I am not yet absolute Mme. Bartolin: he has a claim, and that's all; and perhaps I may find a method to get rid of my master: I have an excellent design in my head: if this handsome Turk has any inclination to me, I am satisfied everything will go well; I am yet mistress of myself, and can terminate all happily: go you, and ask him to dinner: is there any harm in having an agreeable young fellow at one's table, and one that can give good advice, too?

Collette: O excellent advice! nothing can be more proper: let us immediately set about this charitable work.

ACT III.

SCENE I.

Dorfise, Collette.

Dorfise: Is it not he? how uneasy I am! hark! somebody knocks; he's come: Collette, hullo! Collette: 'tis he.

Collette: No, madam, 'tis the chevalier; that impertinent coxcomb, who runs in and out, skips, laughs, prates, and flutters about perpetually; he swears he will have a tête-à-tête with you; and at last, between jest and earnest, I have driven him away.

Dorfise: O send him to my cousin: I hate their insipid parties, their ridiculous prating and nonsense: dear Collette, preserve me from them.

Collette: Hush! hush! I hear somebody coming.

Dorfise: O 'tis my sweet Greek.

Collette: 'Tis he, I believe.

SCENE II.

Dorfise, Adine.

Dorfise: Pray come in: good morrow to you, sir: how I tremble! pray, sir, be seated.

Adine: I'm quite confounded—I beg pardon, madam, I believe, another—

Dorfise: Be not alarmed, sir: I am that other: my cousin dines abroad to-day with Blandford: you must supply his place, and stay with me.

Adine: Supply his place, madam! who can do that? what passion can equal his, or who can exceed him in virtue, honor, and nobleness of soul?

Dorfise: You talk of him with warmth; your friendship has life and spirit in it: I admire you for it.

Adine: 'Tis a sincere regard, but an unhappy one.

Dorfise: Tenderness is to the last degree becoming in youth like thine; virtue is nothing, if it is not linked by the sacred bonds of friendship.

Adine: Alas! if a natural sensibility is the infallible mark of virtue, without vanity, I may boast some degree of worth and honesty.

Dorfise: A soul so noble deserves to be cultivated and improved; perhaps I was born to be the happy instrument; many a woman has long wished in vain to find a tender friend, lively, yet discreet, who possessed all the graces of youth without its flighty extravagance; and, if I am not deceived, in thee all those qualities are united: indeed they are: what lucky star conducted thee to Marseilles?

Adine: I was in Greece, and the brave Blandford brought me from thence; I have told you so twice already.

Dorfise: Suppose you have, I could hear it again and again: but tell me, why is that fair forehead wrapped up in a turban? are you really a Turk?

Adine: Greece is my country.

Dorfise: Who would have thought it? Is Greece in Turkey then? O how I should like to talk Greek with you! why you have all the sprightliness, all the natural ease of a true Frenchman: surely nature mistook when she made you a Greek: well, I bless Providence for throwing you thus amongst us.

Adine: Here I am, to my sorrow.

Dorfise: And canst thou be unhappy?

Adine: Indeed I am so: but 'tis the fault of my own heart.

Dorfise: Ay: 'tis the heart that does all the good and all the evil in this world: 'tis that which makes us both miserable: have you any engagement then?

Adine: I have, indeed: a base intriguing woman has betrayed me: her heart, like her face, is painted and disguised: she is bold, haughty, and full of artifice; more dangerous, because she hides her vices beneath the mask of virtue: how cruel is it that so false a heart should govern one who is but too honest!

Dorfise: Some faithless woman! let us be revenged on her: who is she? of what rank? what country? what is her name?

Adine: That I must not tell you.

Dorfise: Why so? I fear you have art, too, the art of concealment: O you have every talent to please and to delight, young and discreet, beautiful and sensible: but I will explain myself: if, to make you amends for all the injuries you have received, you should meet with a woman rich, amiable, admired, and esteemed; one who had a heart constant, firm, and hitherto untouched, such as is seldom to be met with in Turkey, and more seldom perhaps in this country; if such a one could be found, tell me, sweet youth, what think you? what would you say to her?

Adine: I would say—she meant but to deceive me.

Dorfise: Nay, that would be carrying your distrust too far: come, come, be more confident.

Adine: Forgive me, madam; but the unfortunate, you know, are always a little suspicious.

Dorfise: And what, for example, may your suspicions be whilst I am talking to and looking at you?

Adine: My suspicions are that you mean to try me.

Dorfise: O the malicious little rogue! how cunning he is with that air of innocence: 'tis love himself just out of his childhood: get you gone: I am in absolute danger: positively I'll see you no more.

Adine: Since 'tis your order, madam, I take my leave.

Dorfise: But you need not be in such a hurry to obey: come back, come back, I esteem you too much to be angry with you; but don't abuse my esteem, my sincere regard.

Adine: But you esteem Blandford: can one esteem two at the same time?

Dorfise: O no, never: the laws of reason and of love allow succession, but not division: you'll learn a great deal by living with me, child.

Adine: I have learned a great deal by what I see already.

Dorfise: When heaven, my dear, makes a fine woman, it always at the same time forms a man on purpose for her: we go in search of each other for a long time, and make twenty choices before we fix on the right; we are always looking as it were for our counterpart, and seldom, very seldom, meet with it—by a secret instinct we fly after true happiness; and she [looking tenderly at him] who finds you, need look no further.

Adine: If you knew what I really am, you would soon change your opinion of me.

Dorfise: Never.

Adine: If once you knew me, I'm sure you would think me unworthy, of your care: we should both be caught in the same snare.

Dorfise: Caught, my dear, what can you mean? we're interrupted: O 'tis you, Collette.

SCENE III.

collette, dorfise, adine.

Collette: [In a violent flurry.] Ay, madam, I could not help it; but there's a more impertinent visitor still coming; M. Bartolin.

Dorfise: Indeed! I did not expect him till to-morrow: the villain has deceived me: returned already!

Collette: Ay, madam, and here's another unlucky accident: the chevalier, that king of coxcombs, not knowing the master of the house, is disputing with him in the street, and keeps him there in spite of his teeth.

Dorfise: So much the better.

Collette: No, madam, so much the worse: for this blunderer, not knowing whom he is talking to, laughs in his face, insists upon it that nobody shall come in here to-day; that everybody shall be excluded as well as himself; that he's an impertinent rascal, and that you were engaged in your own apartment in a sober tête-à-tête with a pretty young fellow. Bartolin swears in wrath that he'll break the door down: Mondor splits his sides with laughing, and the other bursts with spleen.

Dorfise: And I in the meantime am dying with fear. O Collette, what shall I do? at what hole shall we creep out?

Adine: What can this mystery be?

Dorfise: The mystery is, that we are both undone: Collette, where are you going?

Adine: What will become of me?

Dorfise: [To Collette.] Hark'ee: stay: what a time was this for him to return! [to Adine] you must hide yourself for tonight in this closet: you'll find a black sack there, wrap yourself up in it, and be quiet. My God! it is he, that's certain.

Adine: [Going into the closet.] O love, what do I suffer for thee!

Dorfise: Poor lad! he's desperately fond of me.

Collette: Hush! hush! here he comes, your dear spouse.

SCENE IV.

Bartolin, Dorfise, Collette.

Dorfise: [Meeting Bartolin.] My dear sir, heaven be with you! how late you are: you made me so uneasy, I was ready to die with fretting.

Bartolin: Mondor told me quite another story.

Dorfise: It's all a lie, every syllable he says, a horrid lie: I think I ought to be believed first; you know I'm sincere: the fellow loves me to madness, and is piqued at my refusal of him: his eternal clack teases me to death: I will positively never see him again.

Bartolin: He seemed to me to talk rationally enough.

Dorfise: Don't believe a word he says.

Bartolin: Well, well, I shan't mind him: I only came to finish our affairs, and to take some necessaries here out of the closet.

Dorfise: [In a persuasive tone.] What are you doing there now? come, don't go into a body's closet.

Bartolin: Why not?

Dorfise: [After pausing a little.] Why, do you know, I had the same thought as you, and have just been putting my papers in order there, so I sent for our old advocate, and we were consulting together, when he was taken with a sudden weakness.

Bartolin: O nothing but old age, he's very old.

Collette: And so, sir, they took him in there to give him

Bartolin: Ay, I understand you.

Dorfise: He's retired a little, and has taken a dose of my syrup: I suppose by this time he has gone to sleep.

Bartolin: That he has not, I am sure, for I hear him walking about and coughing.

Collette: And would you go to disturb an advocate in the midst of his cough?

Bartolin: I don't like this: I'll go in.

Dorfise: Grant heaven he may find nothing there: hark! what do I hear! he cries out; murder! my poor advocate's killed to be sure, and I am undone: which way shall I fly? in what convent shall I hide my shame? where shall I drown myself?

Bartolin: [Returning, and holding Adine by the arm.] O ho! my dear spouse that is to be: your advocates are mighty pretty figures: you have made a good choice, picked him out from the whole bar: come, my old practitioner, you must disappear from this court, and harangue out the window: away with you.

Dorfise: My dear husband, do but hear me.

Adine: He her husband!

Bartolin: [To Adine.] Come, rascal! I must begin my revenge upon you, and curry you out of your insolence.

Adine: Alas! sir, on my knees I ask your pardon; indeed I have not merited your resentment: when you know me, you will lament my fate: I am not what I appear to be.

Bartolin: You appear, my friend, to be a scoundrel, a dangerous rival, and shall be punished: come along, sir.

Adine: Help, here, help! for heaven's sake, sir.

Dorfise: He's mad with passion: help, neighbors, help!

Bartolin: Hold your tongue.

Dorfise, Collette, Adine: Help, here, help!

Bartolin: [Thrusting out Adine.] Come, sir, get out of my house.

SCENE V.

Dorfise, Collette.

Dorfise: What an unfortunate affair this is! he'll kill the poor boy, and me, too, perhaps.

Collette: To be sure, nothing but the devil could make you sign a contract with such a wretch as this.

Dorfise: The villain! go, Collette, this minute, to a justice, and get a warrant for him: charge him with—

Collette: With what, madam?

Dorfise: With everything.

Collette: Very well, madam: but which way are you going?

Dorfise: That I know not.

SCENE VI.

Mme. De Burlet, Dorfise, Collette.

Mme. De Burlet: Why, cousin, cousin, what's the matter?

Dorfise: O cousin!

Mme. De Burlet: One would have thought you'd been robbed and murdered, or that your house had been on fire: what a roaring and a noise there is here, my dear!

Dorfise: O cousin, I'll tell you the affair; but, for heaven's sake, keep my secret.

Mme. De Burlet: I'm no keeper of secrets, cousin; but I can be as discreet as other folks upon occasion: what is this mighty affair of yours?

Dorfise: The affair's a very bad one, I assure you; in short—I am—

Mme. De Burlet: What?

Dorfise: Promised in marriage, cousin.

Mme. De Burlet: I know it, my dear—to Blandford: so much the better: I think it's a good match: I wish you happy, and intend to dance at your wedding.

Dorfise: O my dear, you're mistaken: Bartolin, who is now swearing below stairs, is the man.

Mme. De Burlet: Indeed! so much the worse: I don't approve of your choice; but if it is done, it can't be helped: is he absolutely your husband to all intents and purposes?

Dorfise: Not yet: the world is an utter stranger to it; but the contract has been made a great while.

Mme. De Burlet: O cancel it by all means.

Dorfise: It will set the wicked world talking: O cousin, I have been sadly treated. This vile man, you must know, found me with a young Turk, who was shut up in my closet; not with any bad design.

Mme. De Burlet: O no, to be sure! pray, cousin, is not this a little out of character for a prude?

Dorfise: Not at all: it is a little faux-pas, a small weakness only.

Mme. De Burlet: Well, I am glad you own so much: our faults are sometimes useful: this slip may soften your temper; perhaps for the future you will be less severe.

Dorfise: Severe or not, for heaven's sake, cousin, get me out of this scrape, and save me from the tongue of scandal, and the violence of Bartolin; if possible, deliver the poor lad, who is scarce eighteen. O, here comes my spouse.

SCENE VII.

Bartolin, Dorfise, Mme. De Burlet.

Mme. De Burlet: What an uproar you are making here for nothing! only on a slight suspicion to put all her friends in such a taking: fie, M. Bartolin.

Bartolin: I ask pardon: indeed, ladies, I am ashamed, and sorry I conceived such suspicions; but appearances were strong against her: how indeed could I ever have imagined that this young fellow, for so I thought him, was only a girl in disguise?

Dorfise: [Aside.] An excellent come-off.

Mme. De Burlet: Mighty well indeed! so my lady here took a girl for a boy?

Bartolin: The poor child is in tears still: by my troth, I pitied her: but why could you not have told me who she was? why take a pleasure in trying my temper, and making me angry.

Dorfise: [Aside.] Droll enough this! he has played his part well, however, to persuade Bartolin he is a girl, and get off so well: 'twas a charming contrivance: the dear little rogue! but love is a great wit. [To Bartolin] Now thou abominable jealous wretch, answer me, how dare you thus affront my virtue? the poor little innocent confided in me; my cousin here knows how warmly I espoused her cause, and protected her honor: you ought to have had a loose coquette, a jilt, for your wife; you deserve no better, and I hope you'll meet with one: I'll expose you, sir, though I know it will cost me dear, but I am determined at all events to have the contract annulled.

Bartolin: I know upon these occasions women must cry: but prithee, my dear, don't cry so much: come, let us be friends; and let me desire you, madam, [to Mme.de Burlet] to say nothing about this affair: I have some very good reasons for concealing it.

Dorfise: [To Mme. de Burlet.] Be silent, dear cousin, and save me; on no account mention it to the good M. Blandford.

Mme. De Burlet: You may depend on it, I never will.

Bartolin: We shall be greatly obliged to you.

SCENE VIII.

Dorfise, Mme. De Burlet, Bartolin, Collette.

Collette: M. Blandford is below, madam, and says he must come up.

Dorfise: O dreadful! this is my luck! always crossed—

Bartolin: But after all—

Mme. De Burlet: Nay, nay, after what you have seen, and being guilty of so much injustice as you have, you have no business to give yourself airs: try what you can do—to obey.

SCENE IX.

Dorfise, Mme. De Burlet.

Mme. De Burlet: I'm glad to see this affair has turned out so well, however: to be sure your intended spouse is rather short-sighted: but between you and me, cousin, it was a strange choice this: and then to take a boy for a girl, at his age: well, husbands will be husbands still I find, always jealous, always laughed at, and led by the nose.

Dorfise: [Prudishly.] I don't understand this language, madam, nor have I deserved this treatment from you: surely you don't really believe that a young fellow was locked up in my closet?

Mme. De Burlet: Indeed but I do, my dear.

Dorfise: What! when my husband told you to the contrary?

Mme. De Burlet: Perhaps your spouse might be mistaken; he may have bad eyes: besides, cousin, did you not tell me yourself here in this very place, that a young fellow—

Dorfise: Ridiculous! what I, child, I tell you so? never: do you think I have lost my senses? indeed, cousin, you should take more care what you say: when once a woman's tongue has got a habit of talking thus lightly, and spreading scandalous stories, invented merely to calumniate and injure people, there is no end of it, but 'tis a hundred to one that she repents of it sometime in her life.

Mme. De Burlet: I calumniate, I scandalize you, cousin?

Dorfise: You, madam: I vow and swear—

Mme. De Burlet: Don't swear, cousin.

Dorfise: But I will.

Mme. De Burlet: Fie, my dear, fie: come, come, I shall believe no more of the story than I ought to believe: take a husband, cousin, two if you please; deceive them both as well as you can; make young fellows pass for girls; on the strength of your character govern twenty families, and be called a woman of virtue; with all my heart, it will give me no uneasiness, you are extremely welcome: nay, I admire your management and discretion: 'tis your pride and glory to deceive the world, and mine to divert myself with it, without descending to falsehood: I live for my pleasure: adieu, my dear, my worldly weakness bends in all humility to your profound wisdom: dear cousin, adieu.

SCENE X.

Dorfise, Collette.

Dorfise: Now will that foolish creature go and pull me to pieces: my honor and my character are gone: the libertines will laugh at my expense: Dorfise will be the common butt of every satirist: my name will be hitched into a hundred rhymes, and furnish matter for every singsong in town: Blandford will believe the scandal, and Bartolin will cry for vengeance: how shall I stop the tongues of calumny? two husbands and a lover in one day! what a deal one has to go through to be a prude! would it not be better after all to fear nothing, to affect nothing, and be a plain woman of honor? well: one day or other I'll try to be one.

Collette: At least, madam, let us take care to appear as such; when we do all we can, you know, we have done enough; and she is not always a woman of virtue who wishes to be so.

ACT IV.

SCENE I.

Dorfise, Collette.

Dorfise: O Collette, I'm inevitably ruined: would I could see young Adine; he is so kind, and so sensible! he would tell me everything they do and say, and I might take my measures with him accordingly: my affairs would at least be more settled, and I should know what I have to depend on; what shall I do, Collette?

Collette: See him, and talk to him freely.

Dorfise: Right: towards evening: O Collette, if success would but crown this mysterious affair, if I could preserve my reputation, and keep my lover, if I could but keep one of them, I should be happy.

Collette: Ay, ay, one of them is enough, in conscience.

Dorfise: But have you taken care the chevalier shall be here presently; that he shall come privately; and, according to custom, let everybody know it?

Collette: O never fear, he'll be here I warrant you; he's always ready, and fancies you've a passion for him.

Dorfise: He may be of service: wise men in their designs, the better to compass their ends, always make use of fools.

SCENE II.

Dorfise, Mondor, Collette.

Dorfise: My dear chevalier, come along: I have something to say to you.

Mondor: You know, madam, I am the lowest of your subjects, your humble slave, your chevalier: what must I do? tilt for you? fight for you? die for you? spite of all your cruelty, I am ready: speak, madam, and it is done.

Dorfise: And am I indeed so happy as to have charmed the agreeable Mondor? but do you love me as you ought to love me, with that pure and refined passion?

Mondor: I do; but prithee, my dear, don't be so formal; beauty is most engaging when it is easy and tractable: the excess of virtue is disgusting: in short, my dear, you want a little of my correction.

Dorfise: What think you of young Adine?

Mondor: Who, I? nothing at all? his figure makes me perfectly easy, I assure you: Mars and Hercules were never jealous of Adonis.

Dorfise: Well: I love your confidence, and shall reward it: the malicious world perhaps will tell you I am secretly engaged; but 'tis false; believe them not: a hundred lovers have ogled, and teased me, but I was born to be subdued by you, and you alone.

Mondor: That's more indeed than I could flatter myself with the hopes of.

Dorfise: To convince you of it, I promise to marry you as soon as ever you please: be prudent, and be happy.

Mondor: Happiness is enough for me, prudence we'll leave to another opportunity: but do not, my dear charmer, delay it: time, you know, is precious.

Dorfise: But then one thing I must insist on from you.

Mondor: I am your husband, madam, and you may command me.

Dorfise: You must take care that none of my troublesome visitors intrude on me to-night: the proud, peevish Blandford, my cousin, and her fool Darmin, with all their train of impertinent relations, must go somewhere else, for I positively will not be disturbed by them; then, chevalier, at midnight, and not before, I'll meet you in the arbor; bring your lawyer with you, and we'll sign and seal.

Mondor: Transporting thought! how I shall triumph over that fool Blandford! well, I will so laugh at, so ridicule the poor creature.

Dorfise: Be sure you don't forget to be at my window a little before midnight: away: be discreet.

Mondor: O if Blandford did but know this!

Dorfise: Away, begone, or we shall be surprised.

Mondor: Adieu, my dear wife.

Dorfise: Adieu.

Mondor: I go with rapture, to wait for the dear happy hour when prudery shall be sacrificed to love.

SCENE III.

Dorfise, Collette.

Collette: Well, if I can guess at your design, hang me: 'tis a riddle to me.

Dorfise: I'll explain it to you: I've made Mondor promise to tell nothing, but I know very well he'll tell all, that's enough, his tale will justify me: Blandford will think everything mere calumny, and not know a word of the truth; to-day at least I shall be safe; and after to-morrow, if success crowns my designs, I shall be afraid of nobody.

Collette: Delightful! I'm glad to hear you say so, and yet you put me in a horrid fright: are you sure, ma'am, the plan is well laid? and that you won't, after all, fall into the snare yourself, which you laid for others? for heaven's sake, take care what you do.

Dorfise: O Collette, Collette, how strangely one slip brings on another! we are led aside from error to error, and from crime to crime, till our heads turn round, and we fall down the precipice: but I have one string still to my bow; I am sure of young Adine: the chevalier comes at twelve, but my little lover will be beforehand with him: let him be here at nine, Collette, do you hear me?

Collette: I'll take care of that, madam.

Dorfise: They take him for a girl, by his air, his voice, and his beardless chin; therefore, tell him I would have him dress himself in girl's clothes.

Collette: An excellent scheme! heaven prosper it!

Dorfise: The boy may serve, you know, to dispel one's melancholy: but the great point I would bring about is, to throw all the scandal upon my cousin, and to make Blandford believe that Adine came here upon her account: let him fall a dupe to his own credulity.

Collette: The fittest instrument you could have chosen: for he believes everything that's bad of her, and everything that's good of you: imagines he sees clearly, and at the same time is stark blind: I have taken care already to confirm him in the opinion that our little coquette is in love with the boy, and not you.

Dorfise: To be sure, lies are bad things; but they are mighty serviceable sometimes, and do a great deal of good.

SCENE IV.

Blandford, Dorfise.

Blandford: O tempora! O mores! dreadful corruption indeed! to desire him to visit her! the poor, simple, ingenuous youth, she wants to draw him into a passion for her, and employs all the little subtleties, all the snares which love makes use of to catch unwary hearts.

Dorfise: Well, but after all, M. Blandford, she may not have carried it so far as we imagine: I would not do her so much injury as to suppose it: one should not think evil of one's neighbor: to be sure, things were in a fair way, but you know our French coquettes.

Blandford: Yes, yes, I know them.

Dorfise: The moment a young man appears with an air of innocence and simplicity, they are after him.

Blandford: Yes; yes: vice, above all things, is fond of seducing virtue: but how, Dorfise, can you bear people of such character?

Dorfise: As patiently as I can, sir: but this is not all.

Blandford: Why, what, pray—

Dorfise: O sir, you have another tale to hear: do you know, these excellent contrivers would endeavor to persuade the world truly that the young fellow was brought in for me?

Blandford: For you?

Dorfise: Yes; they say I wanted to seduce him.

Blandford: Well, that to be sure is ridiculous to the last degree: for you!

Dorfise: Ay, for me, and that this pretty youth—

Blandford: That was really a fine invention.

Dorfise: A better than they think for. They have played me a great many such tricks: O M. Blandford, if you knew what I suffer! they'll tell you, too, I'm to be married to that fool, Mondor, and this very night.

Blandford: O my dear Dorfise! the more thou art wounded by the envenomed darts of slander and calumny, with the warmer zeal shall this heart, that adores thee, defend thy injured and unspotted virtue.

Dorfise: You are deceived, indeed you are.

Blandford: No, Dorfise: I think I know myself a little, and I would have laid my life on it I saw your cousin ogling Adine this very day: let me tell you, it requires sense and understanding to be honest: I never knew a fool with a good heart: virtue itself is nothing but good sense: I am sorry for Darmin, because I really love and esteem him; it was against my advice he ventured to embark in such a leaky vessel.

SCENE V.

Blandford, Dorfise, Darmin, Mme. De Burlet.

Mme. De Burlet: What? always dismal and solemn, full of spleen and rancor, grumbling and growling at all mankind, that either don't hear you, or if they do, only laugh at your folly? dear virtuous fool, finish thy soliloquies, and come along with me: I have just bought a few trinkets, you shall have some of them: come, we're going to Mondor's, he's to treat us; I have ordered him to get music, to purge your melancholy humors; and after that, my dear, I'll take you by the hand, and dance with you till to-morrow morning, [to Dorfise] ay, and you shall dance too, Mme. Prim.

Dorfise: Prithee, hair-brains, hold thy tongue: such things would not become me; and besides, madam, you should remember—

Mme. De Burlet: None of your "besides" I beg you, madam: every thing is forgotten; my philosophy is, remember nothing.

Dorfise: [To Blandford.] You see now whether I was right or not: your servant, sir: she really grows too scandalous, I must be gone.

Blandford: O stay, madam.

Dorfise: No, sir: 'tis impossible: it hurts my soul, my honor—

Mme. De Burlet: My goodness! talk less of honor, madam, and regard it more. [Dorfise goes out.]

Darmin: [To Mme. de Burlet.] She seems out of humor: I fancy my friend, Blandford, begins to find her out.

Mme. De Burlet: O all the world must talk of it; but Darmin and I say nothing.

Blandford: I fancy not, indeed: you would hardly confess to me such folly and extravagance.

Darmin: No, sir; we would not make you so unhappy.

Mme. De Burlet: We know your humor too well, to make you still more miserable by reproaching you with your misfortunes.

Blandford: Go, go, hide yourselves both, and die with shame.

Mme. De Burlet: Why should we disturb at once the quiet of your whole life, by exposing Dorfise, and make you a common laughing-stock? no, sir; I own I am light and airy, free, and familiar, but have yet some goodness in me, and am no busybody: I should see you deceived a thousand times by your friend, and duped by your wife, hear your adventures chanted through every street, nay, sing them myself, before ever you should hear a word from me: to tell you the truth, the two great ends I have in view are peace and pleasure; I love myself, and therefore hate all idle reports and scandalous tales, true or false: live and be happy is my motto: and he, I think, is a great fool who makes himself miserable by the follies of others.

Blandford: Light, unthinking woman! it is not the affairs of others, it is your own, madam, that now call for your attention.

Mme. De Burlet: Mine, sir?

Blandford: Yes, madam: 'tis you who are to blame, and highly, too; you who seduced a virtuous youth, and then endeavored to lay the shameful intrigue on the innocent Dorfise.

Mme. De Burlet: O the scheme is excellent: it is more than I expected: and so it was I, who sometimes—

Blandford: Yes, madam, you yourself.

Mme. De Burlet: With Adine!

Blandford: Yes.

Mme. De Burlet: I am in love with him then?

Blandford: Most certainly.

Mme. De Burlet: And 'twas I that put him in the closet?

Blandford: It was: the thing was clear enough.

Mme. De Burlet: O mighty well! a lucky thought indeed! I admire the contrivance: O my dear madman, what a mixture thou art of honesty and folly! the very model of Don Quixote, brave, sensible, knowing, and virtuous, yet in one point an absolute fool; but for heaven's sake take care how you recover your senses: believe me, it would be the worst thing you ever did in your life: well, folly has its advantages: adieu: come, Darmin.

SCENE VI.

Blandford, Darmin.

Blandford: Stay, Darmin, I have your honor and your interest at heart: I am angry, and I have reason to be so; in short, you must quit this artful woman, get out of the snare she has laid for you, despise her, or break with me.

Darmin: The alternative is a cruel one: I own to thee, I love my friend, and I love my mistress: but how can thy hard heart judge so uncharitably of all human kind: can't you see that this web of perfidy is woven by a base, designing woman? that she deceives you, and would lay the shame and ignominy on another?

Blandford: Dost thou not see, fool as thou art, that a vile, scandalous, abandoned wretch has chosen thee for her tool, her butt, her stalking horse, that, like an idiot, you bite at the hook; and that she is only trying to see how far she can exercise her tyranny over your easy heart?

Darmin: Easy as it is, let me entreat you, ask the only witness who is able to determine it: I have sent for young Adine, he will tell you the whole truth of the affair.

Blandford: O yes: I doubt not but the jade has tutored her young parrot well, and taught him his lesson: but let him come, let him endeavor to deceive me;

I shall not believe him: I see your intention, I see plainly enough, you want, by every artifice, to blacken and destroy my dear Dorfise, to draw me off to your niece, whose charms you have so often boasted: but you need not give yourself the trouble, for I shall never think of her.

Darmin: As you please for that: but indeed, Blandford, I pity your folly: to experience the falsehood of a perfidious woman may perhaps be many a poor man's fate, and must be borne; but really to lose one's money is a serious affair: this Bartolin, this noble friend of yours, has he refunded?

Blandford: What business is that of yours?

Darmin: I beg pardon, I thought it was; but I am mistaken: here comes Adine: I'll retire: let me inform you, if you distrust him, you are more in the wrong than you think for: he has a noble heart, and you may one day know he is not what perhaps he might appear to be.

SCENE VII.

Blandford, Adine.

Blandford: So! I see they are all resolutely bent to lead me by the nose: Dorfise, thank heaven, is of another nature; she says nothing, but submits to her unhappy fate without appearing too deeply affected by it; too confident, or too timid; she avoids me, and hides herself in retirement; such is always the behavior of injured innocence. Now, young man, tell me the truth in every particular with sincerity; nature seems in you pure and uncorrupted; you know I love you; do not abuse my growing inclination to you, but consider that the happiness of my life is concerned in this affair.

Adine: Indeed, sir, I love you too well to abuse or to deceive you.

Blandford: Tell me then everything as it passed.

Adine: First then, I assure you, that Dorfise—

Blandford: Stop there, you mean her cousin, I'm sure you do.

Adine: I don't indeed, sir.

Blandford: Well, go on.

Adine: Dorfise then, I say, introduced me by a private door to her chamber.

Blandford: She did, but 'twas not for herself.

Adine: It was.

Blandford: No, child; 'twas Mme. de Burlet, you know it was.

Adine: I tell you, sir, Dorfise was positively in love with me.

Blandford: The little rascal!

Adine: The excess of her passion surprised and shocked me: I was far from being pleased with it: nay, I assure you, I was angry at her: I was incensed at her falsehood; and told her, if I had been like her, I should have been more faithful.

Blandford: The villain! how they have prepared him! well, what followed?

Adine: After this she grew loud and vehement, when on a sudden a violent knocking was heard, and who should come in but her husband.

Blandford: Her husband! O very well! what a ridiculous story! the chevalier, I suppose.

Adine: No: a real husband, I assure you; for he was extremely brutal, and extremely jealous: he threatened to murder her, called her false, perfidious, infamous, and abandoned: I expected to have been killed, too, for he was in a dreadful rage with me, though for what reason I know not: I was forced to fall on my knees and entreat him to spare my life; I'm sure I tremble yet at the thoughts of him.

Blandford: The little coward! but this husband, what was his name?

Adine: I don't know, indeed.

Blandford: A fine trick this!—what sort of a man was he? describe him to me.

Adine: He seemed to me, as far as the horrid fright I was in permitted me to observe him, a fellow of a very disagreeable aspect, fat and short, like a turnspit, flat-nosed, with a large chin, hunch-backed, a yellow-tanned complexion, gray eyebrows, and an eye that looked like—the devil.

Blandford: An excellent picture! how can I recollect him by all this? yellow, you say, tanned, gray, short and fat: who can it be? but you only mean, I see, to laugh at me.

Adine: Try, then, sir, and prove me: to-night, this very night, she has appointed again to meet me.

Blandford: Another appointment with Mme. de Burlet?

Adine: Still, sir, you will mistake the person.

Blandford: Not with Dorfise?

Adine: With her, indeed.

Blandford: With her?

Adine: With her, I tell you.

Blandford: Amazing! you confound me! an assignation with Dorfise this night?

Adine: This very night, sir; if you please, you may see me there: I am to go in girl's clothes, which she herself sent me; and to go in by a private door to your mistress, sir, your faithful, prudent, discreet mistress.

Blandford: This is too much; I cannot, will not bear it: whichever way I consider it, I fear she is disloyal: may I depend upon you?

Adine: My heart is too deeply concerned for your interest and happiness to be insincere: yours I know is truth itself: indeed, M. Blandford, I love, and am faithful to you.

Blandford: The little flatterer!

Adine: Can you doubt my honor?

Blandford: Away! I—

SCENE VIII.

Blandford, Adine, Mondor.

Mondor: Come, come, you make the guests wait, and stop the course of pleasure: why, you never wanted mirth and good company more in your life: to be sure, your affairs go badly enough; you have lost your mistress, but never mind it: you should not have set up for my rival; I told you I should gain the victory, and so I have.

Blandford: What would you inform me of, friend?

Mondor: Nay, nothing of consequence, only that I'm going to be married to your mistress, that's all.

Blandford: O very well! I know that already.

Mondor: What! did you know that I was to carry the lawyer with me, and that—

Blandford: Yes, yes, I know it all, your whole plot, and I don't care a farthing about it: [Aside] This boy has not learned half his lesson; hark'ee, sir, [To Adine] this appointment and yours are a little incompatible: what say you to this, sir? does it strike you? either you endeavor to deceive me, or are deceived yourself: but you are young in the school of vice; a heart like thine, simple and inexperienced, is an excellent instrument in the hands of a villain: alas! thou camest here but to make me miserable.

Adine: This is too much, sir: take care lest your harsh temper, and ill-placed resentment, should destroy that pity which still pleads for you; 'tis that alone which keeps me here: but go, run headlong to your ruin; listen to nobody, suspect your best friend, and believe only those who abuse you; accuse and affront me; but learn to respect a heart that, with regard to you, was never a deceiver, or deceived.

Mondor: Hear you that, sir? but you are choked with spleen; even children laugh at you; prithee, learn to be wiser: come along with me, and drown all your cares in Greek wine: come away, boy.

SCENE IX.

Blandford, Adine.

Blandford: Stay, Adine: thou hast moved me: thy concern alarms me: you know my humor, my folly, but you know my heart too; 'tis honest, and has only too much sensibility: you see how I am distressed; can you take a cruel pleasure in laughing at my misfortunes? tell me the truth, I conjure thee.

Adine: I know your heart is good, nor is mine less pure: never till this hour did I but once put on disguise; but with regard to Dorfise and yourself I have been honest and sincere: I own I lament in you that fatal passion which has blinded you, but 'tis passion I know that will seduce the wisest of us all; love alone can set everything right; that has taken away your sight, and that should restore it to you. [She goes out.]

Blandford: [Alone.] What can he mean? love alone should restore it; he once put on a disguise, and yet he is sincere! I don't understand it; certainly 'tis all a trick, a plot only to make a fool of me: Mondor, Darmin, her cousin, Bartolin, Adine, Dorfise, Collette, all the world in short conspires with my own foolish heart to make me miserable and ridiculous: this vile world, which I despise as it deserves, is nothing but a confused heap of folly and wickedness: but if in this tempest of the soul I must say whether I will be knave or fool, my choice is made, and I bless my lot: O heaven! let me be still a dupe, but O preserve my virtue!

ACT V.

SCENE I.

Blandford: [Alone.] What will become of me? where shall I fly for safety? my misfortunes follow one another without end: I go to sea; a pirate attacks and sinks my vessel: I come to land, and there I am told that an ungrateful woman, whom I adored, is a worse pirate still: a strong box, which I had left behind, is my only resource: a rascal promises to give it me back, and puts me off from time to time, and he perhaps may prove a third corsair: I am waiting for Adine, and he is not come yet; everybody provokes, and everybody avoids me: all perhaps the consequence of my unhappy temper which made me suspicious of every friend, and open to every enemy: if it be so, I am wrong; I own I am, and fortune has a right to sport thus with me: of what service is my melancholy virtue but to make me more sensible to my miseries, and more conscious of having deserved them? this boy, too, not come yet!

SCENE II.

Blandford, Mme. De Burletpassing Across the Stage.

Blandford: [Stopping her.] Stay, madam, I beseech you stay, and calm, if possible, this tempest of my soul; for heaven's sake, one word with you: where are you running to?

Mme. De Burlet: To supper: to be merry: I'm in haste, sir.

Blandford: I know I affronted you, and you have reason to be angry; but forget and forgive.

Mme. De Burlet: [Smiling.] O I have forgiven you a great while ago: I'm not angry, I assure you.

Blandford: You are too good: will your gayety for once deign to interest itself in my distress?

Mme. De Burlet: Gay as I am, M. Blandford, I assure you, I have friendship, esteem, and pity for you.

Blandford: You are sorry, then, for my unhappy fate.

Mme. De Burlet: Your unhappy fate! yes: but more for your unhappy temper.

Blandford: You are honest, however, and truth you know, has always charms for me: but say, is Darmin a faithful friend, or does he deceive me?

Mme. De Burlet: Darmin loves you, and possesses all your virtues with more softness and complacency.

Blandford: And Bartolin?

Mme. De Burlet: You want me to answer for Bartolin, too, and for all the world, I suppose: excuse me; Bartolin, for aught I know, is an honest cashier; what reason have you to suspect him? he's your friend, and the friend of—Dorfise.

Blandford: Of Dorfise? but tell me freely; could Dorfise, could she entertain a passion for a boy, and in so short a time, too? and what is this lawyer that Mondor talks of? public report says he's to marry her.

Mme. De Burlet: Public reports should be despised.

Blandford: I am this moment come from her: she has sworn eternal truth to me: she has wept: love and grief were in her eyes: did they belie her heart? is she false? and is Adine—you laugh at me.

Mme. De Burlet: I laugh at your ridiculous figure: come, come, take courage, man: as for the boy, take my word for it, he'll never forsake you; 'tis impossible.

Blandford: You give me comfort: the coxcomb, Mondor, is not worth my care; Dorfise loves me, and I love her forever.

Mme. De Burlet: Forever? that's too much.

Blandford: Not where one is beloved; but then this Adine must be a base calumniator, must have a bad heart.

Mme. De Burlet: O no: be assured, he has a noble mind, candid, honest, and ingenuous, the happy favorite of indulgent nature.

Blandford: You mock me, madam.

Mme. De Burlet: Indeed I don't: 'tis truth.

Blandford: Now am I plunged again in darkness and uncertainty; you sport with my distress, and take pleasure in tormenting me: Dorfise, or he, has deeply injured me: one of them, you must allow, has been a traitor to me; is it not so?

Mme. De Burlet: [Laughing.] That may be.

Blandford: If it is, you see what reason I had—

Mme. De Burlet: And after all it may not be so: I accuse nobody.

Blandford: I'll be revenged.

Mme. De Burlet: Ridiculous! be less angry and more discreet: come, I'll tell you what; will you take the only sure method, one that I shall recommend to you?

Blandford: I will.

Mme. De Burlet: Then leave this dark mysterious affair to itself; make no bustle about it, but turn everything, as I do, into a jest; take your money from Bartolin, and live along with us without care or solicitate: never go too deeply into things, but float with me upon the surface; you know the world, and bear with it; the only way to enjoy is to skim lightly over it: you look upon me as a giddy creature, and so I am; but let me tell you, the only matter of importance in this life is to enjoy ourselves, and be happy.

SCENE III.

Blandford: [Alone.] To be happy! good! excellent advice! would not one think now it were an easy thing; that one had only to wish for happiness, to possess it? would it were so! and why should it not be? why should I take so much pains to make myself unhappy? shall I suffer this boy, and Darmin, and Mondor to distract me thus? no: I'll follow this giddy girl's advice; she's gay, but honest and sincere: Dorfise loves me, and I am yet secure: for the future, I'll see nothing, listen to nothing: they wanted to alarm me with this Adine, to hoodwink, and then to lead me where they pleased; but I'm not to be caught in their snares: Darmin is wrapped up in that niece of his, and would fain palm her upon me; but I detest her: ha! what's this? [Adine appears in woman's clothes at the farther end of the stage.]

Yonder's that unhappy youth who has caused me so much uneasiness: he looks exactly like a girl: how genteel his air, and so easy, too, as if the clothes had been made for him! the face is too truly female.

SCENE IV.

Blandford, Adine.

Adine: Well, sir, you see I'm dressed for my part, and now you will know the truth.

Blandford: I desire to know nothing more about it! I have heard enough; leave me, I beseech you; I have altered my sentiments, and hate this disguise; go, go, put on your own habit, and trouble yourself no more with this affair.

Adine: What say you, sir? at last then I perceive it is not in my power to change your unalterable heart, or to reverse your cruel fate; alas! you know not the weight of grief that hangs upon me, but ere long you will see the fatal effect of it: farewell! I leave you, sir, forever.

Blandford: What can this mean? he weeps! speak, I entreat thee, tell me, what interest hast thou in my happiness or misery?

Adine: My interest, sir, was yours: till this moment never knew I any other: but I have been to blame, I tried to serve you; 'tis not the first time.

Blandford: The innocence of his look, his modest confidence, his voice, his air, his open and ingenuous behavior, still plead for him—but the hour is past when this intrigue you told me of was to have taken place; I was to have been an eye-witness of it.

Adine: Hark! I hear a door opening: this is the place, and this the time, when you shall be convinced who it is that loves you.

Blandford: Just heaven! it is possible?

Adine: It is.

Blandford: Stay you here then: but 'tis all a trick, an artifice: Dorfise! no—

Adine: Hush! I hear a noise: it comes towards us: I'm frightened, 'tis so dark.

Blandford: Fear nothing.

Adine: Be silent: for I hear somebody coming: hush! away.

SCENE V.

Adine, Blandford, on One Side of the Stage, Which Is Supposed to Be Quite Dark; dorfise on the Other, on Tiptoe.

Dorfise: I thought I heard my charmer's voice; how punctual he is! the dear boy.

Adine: Hush!

Dorfise: Hush, is it you?

Adine: Yes: 'tis I: still faithful to my love: 'tis I who come here to prove that I have deserved a better return for all my tenderness.

Dorfise: I cannot give thee a better: you must forgive me; I would not have made you wait so long, my dear, but Bartolin, whom I did not expect, is returned: in spite of all my care, he has got a fit of jealousy upon him.

Adine: Perhaps he is afraid of meeting Blandford here: he is a dangerous rival.

Dorfise: Very likely, indeed: O my dear, what with Blandford, and my vile husband, I'm dreadfully hampered: I don't know which I hate most: in short, I'm sure of nothing, but that I love you.

Adine: You hate Blandford then heartily?

Dorfise: I think I do: fear naturally begets aversion.

Adine: Well, but your other spouse—

Dorfise: O him I never think of.

Blandford: [Aside.] How I could wish now—

Adine: [Softly to Blandford.] Hush! hush!

Dorfise: I have been consulting, my dear, about the contract: it certainly might be set aside: I wish it were, and then I might have hopes of another match.

Adine: What, of marrying me?

Dorfise: I think the best way would be for us to part for a time, to avoid scandal; and then meet, and be united by a sacred and a lasting tie.

Adine: A lasting tie! come then: let us begone: but how are we to live?

Dorfise: Your prudent foresight charms me: I always admired your discretion: you must know, then, the fighting M. Blandford, a hero at sea, but an arrant blockhead at home, when he left Marseilles, to go after the pirates, most cordially and most affectionately consigned to me with his heart, his money and jewels also: as I was, like him, a novice in these affairs, I put them into the hands of my other husband; from him I must endeavor to recover them, and assist

Blandford: the poor man is honest and should live: away: let us part immediately, and take care nobody follows us.

Adine: But what will the world say?

Dorfise: O never heed it: I was afraid of its scandal before I loved: but now I despise it: I'll be a slave to none but thee.

Adine: But me?

Dorfise: I'll go immediately and get this strong box: that you know will be very necessary to us both: stay here, I'll be back in an instant.

SCENE VI.

Blandford, Adine.

Adine: Well, sir, what think you now?

Blandford: Never did I behold such base, such black ingratitude, such infernal falsehood; and yet, Adine, you see the force of powerful virtue, how its lively instinct speaks even in the most corrupted heart.

Adine: How, sir, in what?

Blandford: You see the perfidious wretch dared not rob me of all; she talked of assisting me.

Adine: [Ironically.] O yes, you are mightily obliged to her: have you not another strong box to intrust with this virtuous lady?

Blandford: Nay, do not laugh at me, Adine, nor plant such daggers in my heart.

Adine: I meant to heal and not to wound it: but can you yet admire her?

Blandford: No: she is loathsome: falsehood has robbed her of every charm.

Adine: If, sir, I free you from her snares, may I flatter myself, that while you detest her vices, you will not forget my honest service?

Blandford: No, generous youth! I look on you as my son and my deliverer, the guardian angel, whom heaven hath sent down to preserve me; the half of all I have will be but a poor reward for thy care and fidelity.

Adine: You must not know at present what reward I aspire to: but can your heart refuse the request which Darmin perhaps may ask of you?

Blandford: Ha! thou hast removed the veil: I see, I see it all; but who, what art thou? art thou indeed what thou resemblest?

Adine: [Smiling.] Whatever I am, for heaven's sake, be silent now: I hear Dorfise coming this way.

Dorfise: [With strong box.] I've got the box; propitious love has favored my design: here, my dear, take it: away: let us be gone: have you got it fast?

Blandford: [Taking it from her, and counterfeiting the voice of Adine.] Yes.

Dorfise: Come along then.

SCENE VII.

blandford, dorfise, adine, bartolin with a sword in his hand, in the dark, he runs up to Adine.

Bartolin: Stop, villain, stop! art thou not satisfied with robbing me of my wife, but must run away with my money, too?

Adine: [To Blandford.] Help! murder! help!

Blandford: [Fighting with one hand, and holding out the box to Adine with the other.] Take the box.

SCENE VIII.

Blandford, Dorfise, Adine, Bartolin, Darmin, Mme. De Burlet, Collette, Mondor with a Napkin and a Bottle in His Hand. Flambeaux.

Mme. De Burlet: What's the matter here! hui! hui! what! fighting, too?

Mondor: Hold, hold, gentlemen, what is all this noise about?

Adine: [To Blandford.] You're not wounded, sir, I hope?

Dorfise: [In confusion.] Ha!

Mme. De Burlet: What is the cause of this fray, gentlemen? pray inform us.

Blandford: [To Bartolin, after disarming him.] O nothing, madam; only this worthy gentleman, and trusty treasurer, this honest keeper of the strong box, had robbed me of my mistress and my fortune: by the assistance of this amiable youth, I have detected their infamous designs, and recovered my money: go, sir, I leave you to your miserable fate, to this virtuous lady: know, my friends, I have unmasked their treacherous hearts; this villain—

Bartolin: [Going off.] Your servant, sir.

Mondor: A ha! what comes of my assignation now?

Blandford: O, sir, they made a fool of you.

Darmin: And of you too, I think.

Blandford: They did so, indeed: I feel it yet.

Mondor: Treated you like an idiot.

Blandford: Dreadful, horrible! O prudery, how I detest thee!

Mondor: Well, come, let us think no more of prudes, wives, or women, but go in and drink about; that's my way of drowning misfortunes: the man that drinks is never melancholy.

Mme. De Burlet: I'm really sorry my cousin Dorfise should behave so foolishly: to be sure, it will set the world to talking, but it will be all over soon, and there's an end of it.

Darmin: Come, Blandford, banish sorrow, and for the future take care of a prude: but do you know this boy, who has restored to you your honor and fortune, and saved you from the dangerous precipice which your blind passion had led you to the brink of?

Blandford: [Looking at Adine.] But—

Darmin: 'Tis my niece.

Blandford: O heaven!

Darmin: The very woman whom I so often proposed to my deluded friend; who, deceived by a faithless wretch, despised and hated all but her.

Blandford: How could I injure, by an unkind refusal, so many charms! such beauty and such virtue!

Adine: You never would have known me, if chance and my own constancy had not removed the veil of black ingratitude, and saved you from yourself.

Darmin: You owe everything, your fortune, and your reason to her generous love: what, then, is she to hope for in return? what will you do to make her amends?

Blandford: [Kneeling to Adine.] Adore her!

Mondor: This turn of affairs is as agreeable as it is surprising: we shall all be gainers by the change: away.

End

www.ingramcontent.com/pod-product-compliance
Lightning Source LLC
Chambersburg PA
CBHW031421040426
42444CB00005B/671